Growing Girls With Curls

Short Stories For Girls Of Color

Chantal Maples

Growing Girls With Curls

Copyright © 2018 Chantal Maples
All rights reserved. Printed in the United States of America. No part of this book may be used or reproduced in any manner whatsoever without written permission except in the case of brief quotations in critical articles or reviews.

<u>For more information contact:</u>
Chantal Maples
growinggirlswithcurls@gmail.com
www.growinggirlswithcurls.com

Typesetting, Book Layout, Editing and Cover Design by Enger Lanier Taylor
for In Due Season Publishing

Published By: In Due Season Publishing
　　　　　　　Huntsville, Alabama
　　　　　　　indueseasonpublishing@gmail.com
　　　　　　　www.indueseasonpublishing.com

ISBN-13: 978-0999238759
ISBN-10: 0999238760

Presented To:

_____

Dedication

I dedicate this book to Aubrey and Courtlynn, my two growing girls with curls. You girls bring out all of the best parts of me.
Mommy loves you so much.

I also dedicate this to my mom, Regina Slay, who has always supported me and
Enger Lanier-Taylor who made this book possible.
Thank you both from the
bottom of my heart.

Table of Contents

Growing Girls With Curls

Black Girl Magic

My Mom is A Superhero

Wash Day

Aubrey

Courtlynn

GROWING GIRLS WITH CURLS

My hair is curly, big, and round.
My sister's is black, mine sandy brown.
Please do not touch, or I will frown.
Full of glory is this crown.

My hair is curly, my sister's is too!
Buns, braids, and twistouts is
what we like to do.
Sometimes, it is unruly, other
times it is neat.
My curly hair is what makes me unique.

Our hair is curly, this is true.
We can rock any style we choose.
It makes us stand out from all of
the other girls.
I am Courtlynn, she is Aubrey,
two growing girls with curls.

BLACK GIRL MAGIC

It is the way we look and style our hair that makes people pay attention.
They stop and stare.
It is our brown skin, full lips, and our natural glow.
Magic beaming from our heads all the way down to our toes.

With our style and confidence, we set the standard high.
Our strength, courage, and resilience you cannot deny.
Magical we are, and will always be.
Black girl magic is real; black girl magic is me!

MY MOM IS A SUPERHERO

My mom is a superhero, the strongest person I know.
She does everything for me and my sister.
If she is tired, it does not show.
She does the cooking and cleaning and helps with homework too.
My mom is a superhero; there is nothing she can't do.

My mom is a superhero.
That much is a fact.
She is there for me when I need her.
I know she will always have my back.
I can talk to her about anything, all problems big and small.
My mom is the best mom ever, for me she does it all.

My mom is a superhero.
I am telling you that it is true.
She says I can grow up to be anything, and
I believe her too.
An engineer or a doctor;
anything that I choose.
With my mom standing beside me,
there is no way that I can lose.

Our mom is a superhero.
Our favorite girl in the world.
We appreciate everything she does for us,
her two growing girls with curls.

WASH DAY

Today is wash day, and you
know what that means.
It is time to shampoo my hair and get
my scalp all nice and clean.
Hot oil treatments, deep conditioning,
and hair masks
are part of the routine.
I look forward to wash day, I get
pampered like a Queen.

Today is wash day, and I am upset.
I do not want to be still; I do not
want my hair wet.
Do not detangle my hair;
just throw it up in a bun.
No, I do not like wash day.
For me, it is not fun!

Today is wash day, and
I am tired to the max.
My hands are cramping; I just
need to relax. With two curly girls,
this is an all-day affair.
My two growing girls with curls, and
their ever growing hair.

Today was wash day, and
we are finally done.
Our hair is clean and conditioned;
laced with beads, braids, and beyond.
Wash day is different for every little girl.
Thank God, we are finished.

Sincerely,

Two Growing Girls with Curls

Aubrey & Courtlynn

About the Author

Chantal Maples is a young mother of two, born and raised in Huntsville, Alabama. Chantal is a lifestyle and natural hair blogger who encourages young women to embrace their natural hair while facing life's challenges head on. You can follow and join the Growing Girls with Curls community at www.growinggirlswithcurls.com. You can also follow along on Facebook, Pinterest - @growinggirlswithcurls
Instagram - Growinggirlstv

www.ingramcontent.com/pod-product-compliance
Lightning Source LLC
Chambersburg PA
CBHW060809090426
42736CB00003B/212